CONTENTS

FISHING

People have been fishing for tens of thousands of years to catch food to eat. The sport of fishing with a **rod**, line and hook is called **angling**. It is different from fishing with large nets to catch fish for food. Angling is popular all over the world, because it is a wonderful way to connect with nature and enjoy an adventure in the great outdoors.

There are three types of angling. The first is sea fishing, in which you catch saltwater fish from a boat or the seashore. The second is game fishing. This is catching salmon or trout. The third type is coarse fishing. This is catching other **freshwater** fish and it is the most popular fishing sport today. This book tells you all about this type of fishing.

There is nothing quite like the satisfaction of catching a fish!

Adventures in the
GREAT OUTDOORS

FISHING

Robyn
Hardyman

raintree

Raintree is an imprint of Capstone Global Library Limited, a company incorporated in England and Wales having its registered office at 264 Banbury Road, Oxford, OX2 7DY – Registered company number: 6695582

www.raintree.co.uk
myorders@raintree.co.uk

Produced for Raintree by Calcium
Edited by Sarah Eason and Katie Woolley
Designed by Emma DeBanks
Picture research by Sarah Eason
Production by Victoria Fitzgerald
Originated by Capstone Global Library Ltd © 2016
Printed and bound in China

ISBN 978 1 4747 1549 2 (hardback)
19 18 17 16 15
10 9 8 7 6 5 4 3 2 1

ISBN 978 1 4747 1552 2 (paperback)
20 19 18 17 16
10 9 8 7 6 5 4 3 2 1

British Library Cataloguing in Publication Data
A full catalogue record for this book is available from the British Library.

Acknowledgements
We would like to thank the following for permission to reproduce photographs: Shutterstock: Alexnika 4, Arena Creative 14b, Auremar 8, Blend Images 21, CCat82 25, Norman Chan 13l, D7INAMI7S 26t, Goodluz 1, 19, Gorillaimages 18, Imageman 15, Kaczor58 14t, Kletr 10, Kzww 12, Petr Malyshev 13r, Michaeljung 16, Monkey Business Images 5, Susan Montgomery 7, Paul B. Moore 6, Mountainpix 23, Oliveromg 9, Panbazil 26b, Pinponpix 17, Regina Pryanichnikova 20, Galushko Sergey 11, Bjorn Stefanson 29, Tab62 22, Cappi Thompson 28, Txking 24, Nikitin Victor 26c, 27t, Edward Westmacott 27b.

Cover photographs reproduced with permission of: Shutterstock: Matt Jeppson.

Every effort has been made to contact copyright holders of material reproduced in this book. Any omissions will be rectified in subsequent printings if notice is given to the publisher.

Some words are shown in bold, **like this**. You can find out what they mean by looking in the glossary.

STAY SAFE!

Deep water can be dangerous. Always fish with an adult and be careful near water.

Adult anglers will be happy to pass their fishing knowledge and experience on to you.

You can go fishing at any age. You just need some basic equipment, a love of being outdoors and plenty of patience. You may have to wait a while for a fish to bite, but it is worth the wait when you feel a tug on the line and you **reel** in your catch. It feels great when you land your own fish! If you get hooked on fishing, you could even join a local club. Clubs hold competitions and you will get to talk to other anglers about your favourite sport, too.

PLAN YOUR TRIP

To make the most of your fishing trip, you need to do some planning before you go. There is a lot to think about and some important questions to ask before your trip.

One of the most important questions is whether you need a **licence** to fish. Children under the age of 12 do not usually need a rod licence, but the adult you are with will need one. You can buy a rod licence online from the Environment Agency or at the Post Office. The Environment Agency can also tell you the local fishing regulations.

It is important to know fishing regulations and to follow the rules. Fishing is not allowed at certain times of year, because the fish are laying their eggs. Preventing fishing at these times means the supply of fish is protected for the future. You may also need permission to fish in your chosen location from the landowner or local fishing club.

Do not forget to take something to sit on and the right clothing for the weather. This includes a hat to protect you from the sun or rain.

FISHING LOG BOOK

Make a fishing log to record your successes.

1 Decide the type of information you want to record, such as the date and time of the trip, location, weather and who you are fishing with.

2 Decide what you want to record about your catch, such as species of fish and its weight.

3 Plan how you want to write the information in your log book.

4 Pack a camera to take photographs of your fish.

5 Take some portable weighing scales, to weigh your catch.

EXPLORE THIS!

You will need:
- hardcover notebook
- camera
- portable weighing scales

CATCH AND RELEASE

SELECTIVE RELEASE

RECYCLE THE BIG ONES

STAY SAFE! Remember to take a first aid kit for any cuts or grazes.

Remember to follow the signs wherever you are fishing.

GET THE GEAR

You cannot catch fish without some essential tackle, or equipment. The most essential pieces of tackle are the fishing rod and reel.

There are different rods for catching different types of fish. Start with a general purpose rod, around 1.5 metres (5 feet) long. It should be light enough to be comfortable for you to hold. This type of rod has sections, which you fit together and line up.

The **spool** that holds the line faces towards the rod's tip.

A lever called the **bail arm** holds the line on the reel.

The reel is for holding the line and wheeling it in and out of the water.

REEL AND LINE

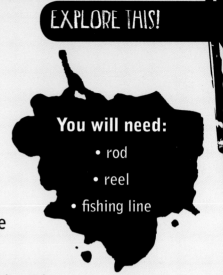

You will need:
- rod
- reel
- fishing line

This is how to attach the reel and line to your rod.

1 Slide the reel fittings on the rod over the butt of the reel.

2 Hold out the rod with the reel on the underside, facing the ground. Open the bail arm on the reel.

3 Unwind about 1 metre (3 feet) of line and tie one end to the reel's spool with a knot. Wrap it around a few times, then close the bail arm.

4 Turn the handle of the reel away from you. This makes the bail arm spin and the line slide onto the spool.

5 Stop turning when the line has filled up the spool. Cut the line.

6 Turn the reel handle towards you to unwind the line. Thread the end of the line through the rings along the length of the rod.

A spinning reel is suitable for all types and sizes of fish.

HOOKS AND KNOTS

It is the hook at the end of the line that catches hold of the fish's mouth. To catch different fish, you will need to know which types of hook to use and how to tie them onto your line.

Remember to match the size of the hook to the size of the fish you are likely to catch. If the hook is too small, the fish could swallow it. If a fish does swallow a hook, you can remove it with a special hook-removal tool. If the hook is too big, the fish will not bite.

One end of the hook has a small eye. This is where you tie the hook to your line. To do this, you will need to know how to tie fishing knots. The fishing line is a thin, see-through wire. When tying any knot, always wet the line with water to make it slippery.

STAY SAFE!

Hooks are sharp! Handle them with care and always hold the line above the hook if possible.

*Some fish hooks have a **barb** on them. This is difficult to remove from a fish's mouth, so always use hooks without barbs.*

KNOTTY BUSINESS

Learn to tie a **cinch knot**, which is perfect for tying the hook to the line.

You will need:
- hook
- some line

1 Pass the line through the hook's eye twice, making a large loop.

2 Wrap the end of the line around the main line four or five times.

3 Now pass the free end of the line through the big double loop near the eye end of the line.

4 Wet the line and pull the end tightly to close the knot.

*A hook and a **fly** are attached by a knot to this fishing line.*

FISH BAIT

To catch fish, you need to tempt them with something tasty to eat! This is the bait. Choosing the right bait is one of the main skills of fishing.

Live fish eat live food, so it is easy to see why they prefer live bait. Live bait includes worms, grubs and insects. The downside of using live bait is that you have to keep the bait alive. Grubs, for example, last only about one week if you keep them cool. However, you can use food such as pieces of cheese, small balls of bread and corn instead of live bait.

Anglers often use artificial bait instead of live bait. Flies are made from feathers, fur and wire, so they look like insects. **Lures** are made from wood, plastic or metal, to look like small fish. Both flies and lures have a hook.

Fishing flies such as these are designed to look like insects.

WORMS FOR BAIT

Find worms and attach them correctly onto your line.

You will need:
- small implement for digging, such as a trowel
- small plastic box with a lid
- hook

1 On the riverbank, dig in a patch of soil to find some worms.

2 Put some soil in the plastic box and store your worms inside it.

3 Attach a worm to your hook by pushing the hook all the way through its body.

4 Push the hook through the middle of the worm. That way, the worm will wriggle at both ends.

Light-coloured lures are best for clear water.

You can even use sweets such as jellybeans for bait!

13

FLOATS AND SINKERS

In some situations, you will want to use either a float or a sinker (weight) on your line plus the bait.

Floats are used when you are trying to catch fish near the surface of the water. Floats are round or oblong shapes made of plastic and are attached to the line above the hook and bait. They sit on the surface. When floats move or disappear, it is a sign that you have got a bite! Floats are great for shallow, calm water.

Sinkers do the opposite job to floats. They are heavy and are used to catch fish near the bottom of the water. Sinkers are threaded onto the line and drag it down. They come in different shapes for use in different types of water.

The hook with the bait is deep down in the water, below the float.

*Use a **tackle box** to keep your kit organized. There are a lot of compartments for keeping floats, sinkers, hooks, bait and line.*

14

SETTING UP THE FLOAT

Get your float set up just right on the line.

You will need:
- line, hook and bait
- float and float ring
- split shot

1 Slide the float ring onto the line about 1 metre (3 feet) from the end and push the bright end of the float through the ring.

2 Thread the line through the eye at the other end of the float.

3 Attach the hook and bait to the end of the line.

4 Squeeze three **split shot** onto the line, a few centimetres apart.

5 **Cast** the line into the water. Only the top of the float should be visible on the surface.

Split shot are small weights that hold down the hook and make the float sit upright.

STAY SAFE! Do not use floats if ducks or swans are on the water. They will go for the bait and get caught on the hook.

You are now ready to choose the perfect place to cast your line. So, where are the fish?

You will need to do a bit of detective work to find fish. Look for clues such as bubbles or ripples in the water. Undisturbed areas, below overhanging trees or in weeds, are often good places to find fish. Avoid anywhere many boats pass by because they are likely to disturb the fish.

You can cast, or throw your line, underarm or overhead. Either way, it is all about timing and releasing the line at exactly the right moment to make sure you put the bait where you want it without making a big splash. Underarm casting is best if there are trees, bushes or power cables around you.

If you use overhead casting, your bait will travel further.

OVERHEAD CASTING

You will need:
- fishing rod and line, set up with hook and bait

Here is how to master an overhead cast.

1 In one hand, hold the rod almost upright.

2 Turn the handle to wind in the line until it hangs a third of the way down the rod.

3 With your finger, press the line coming off the reel up against the rod handle. Then open the bail arm.

4 Swing the rod back a little bit, then quickly push away with your top hand and pull down with your bottom hand.

5 Straighten your top arm, then take your finger off the line. The line will fly forwards into the water.

STAY SAFE!

Do not cast from slippery places. Stay at least 100 metres (110 yards) from any overhead power cables.

It takes a little practice to master overhead casting.

17

YOU HAVE A BITE!

You feel a pull on the line, and you have got a bite! Now you need to get your fish out of the water before it escapes. If it is a good size, it will try to swim away. The trick is to let the fish get tired, so it will be easier to land.

To tire out the fish, make sure the hook is firmly in the fish's mouth. Reel in any slack line and sharply raise the tip of your rod. A big fish, struggling hard, will break the line and get away, so let out some line.

The rod tip will bend as the fish swims away from you. As it swims back towards you, lift the rod tip up to tighten the line and reel it in slowly. Do this several times. Each time, you are bringing the fish closer to the bank and tiring it out. Be patient, the fish is almost yours!

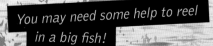

You may need some help to reel in a big fish!

STAY SAFE!

Make sure you are standing on firm ground as you reel in a fish. A big fish pulling hard on the line could pull you into the water if you are on slippery rocks.

Keep a close eye on your fish as you bring it in.

You need to act fast when you are about to catch a fish. This is especially true in summer, when the fish are more active. In winter, they may not move towards the bait as quickly. Then you may have to wait a few seconds more. You will learn from experience. When the fish get away with your bait, you will see how fast you have to be!

19

LAND IT!

Landing your fish is the most exciting part of any fishing trip. It is really important not to give up now. Remember to use the right landing techniques to make sure you get your fish!

By now you should have tired out your fish and brought it close to the bank. Lower the end of your rod to keep the fish under the water. Bring it to the edge by turning the reel handle away from you to shorten the line. Now lift the rod tip upwards again. You will need another person to hold the landing net. That person should slide the net under the fish as you hold up the rod tip to keep the line tight. Gradually tighten the line further, while the other person lifts the net out of the water.

Have your landing net ready to take the fish as you land it.

It is a proud moment when a fish is finally yours.

If you are landing a small fish, you can just bring it in towards the bank. Now lift the tip of your rod until you see the fish come out of the water. With one hand, hold the rod steady and swing the line towards you. Catch hold of the fish with your other hand. Well done, you are a real angler now!

STAY SAFE!

Try to hold the line above the fish so you do not get hurt by the sharp hook.

HANDLING FISH

You have got your fish! You now need to decide whether to keep it or release it back into the water. Either way, you will want to weigh and record it first. You will need to act quickly to make sure that the fish is unharmed.

Always make sure that your hands are wet when you pick up a fish. Otherwise you can remove some of the layer of slime that protects it. Firstly, remove the hook from the fish's mouth. If you can see it, carefully turn it and slide it out. If it is deep inside the mouth, you will need a special tool to remove it. If it is too deep to remove, cut the line and leave it in the fish. Some hooks will simply dissolve or fall out after a while.

Record your catch with a camera and the weighing scales.

Fish can take a few seconds to get used to being back in the water.

Take a photo of your fish for your records. To find the weight, attach the landing net with the fish inside it to your portable scales. You can weigh the empty net later, and subtract that number from your result to find the weight of the fish. You can measure your fish, too, and record it in your log book.

Try to cause the fish as little distress as possible. If you are returning it to the water, do so quickly. To let it recover from the shock of being caught, hold it gently underwater for a few seconds. When its **gills** are moving strongly, let it go.

STAY SAFE! The fins and gills of a fish can be surprisingly sharp, so be careful when you handle it.

COOK IT!

Part of the fun of fishing is eating what you have just caught. Check first that the rules of your fishing ground allow you to cook the fish on the land where you caught it.

It is great to cook your fish whole, but you need to remove the guts first. Ask an adult to help you do this because you will need to use a sharp knife. Wash out the insides of the fish with cold water. Do not worry about the scales. Once the fish is cooked, you will remove the skin and the scales with it.

A lot of the fish's flavour is in the skin, so it is best to leave it on.

FISH DISH

Try this great recipe for your fresh fish.

1 Clean the fish by gutting and rinsing it.

2 In a bowl, mix the chopped onion, lemon juice, herbs, salt and pepper.

3 Stuff each fish with some of the herby onion mixture.

4 Wrap each fish in one or two bacon slices.

5 Wrap each fish in a piece of foil and place on a hot grill over the fire for at least 15 minutes. The cooking time depends on the size of your fish.

6 Check that the flesh of the fish is cooked through thoroughly.

7 Unwrap the cooked fish and remove the skin.

You will need, for four people:

- 4 freshly-caught fish
- 1 medium onion, finely chopped
- 6–8 slices of bacon
- juice of 1 lemon
- rosemary, thyme, salt and pepper
- foil

Many people cook their fish whole on a grill over an open fire.

25

WHAT IS ON THE LINE?

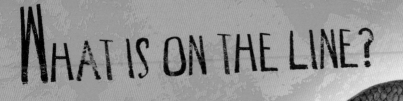

carp

The rivers, streams and lakes of the United Kingdom are teeming with fish. With so many fish around, it is good to know what might end up on your line.

Fish that live in rivers, lakes and streams are called freshwater fish because the water there is not salty. Some of the most popular freshwater fish for anglers are pike, carp, bream, gudgeon, roach, perch, trout and tench. Roach is found almost everywhere, in rivers, canals, ponds and lakes. Their lower fins are red, which has led to their nickname "redfin". You will need a fine line and a small float to catch a roach. Use maggots or maggot pupae as bait, which a roach loves to eat, but you will have to reel your catch in quickly before it swims away with your bait!

perch

roach

pike

Pike live all across the United Kingdom. They are easily recognizable by their torpedo-shaped striped or spotted bodies. They eat other fish and their mouths are full of backwards-pointing, razor-sharp teeth. You need a powerful rod and a strong line to catch a pike. Trout can live in flowing and still water. They like to be near cover such as underwater rocks, or beneath overhanging bushes. You are most likely to catch a trout in the late afternoon or early evening when they are out and about actively feeding. Fly fishing for trout is very popular, especially in Scotland.

trout

GO GREEN

We all have a responsibility to keep our countryside safe and unspoilt for the future. That way, everyone can continue to enjoy it. Wherever you are fishing, it is important to remember to respect the natural environment and make as little impact on it as you can.

Anglers need to be very aware of wildlife, because the equipment they use can cause harm. Never leave tangles of line on the ground for birds and other animals to get caught up in. Hooks are dangerous, too. Do not leave them around with bait on, as they could tempt small creatures. Use barbless hooks because they cause less damage to the fish. Remember that other animals use the rivers and lakes, too. Bring in your line if there is a risk of birds swimming through it and getting snared.

Carefully pack up everything you brought with you.

After a perfect fishing trip, try to leave no trace behind.

The rules of clubs and landowners are there for a reason, so respect them. Do not catch more than you are allowed and release the fish if that is required. This preserves fish stocks for everyone.

When it is time to go, pack up everything, including your rubbish, and take it home with you. The idea is to leave nothing behind!

GLOSSARY

angling sport of fishing

bail arm lever on the reel that holds the line in place

bait piece of food put onto the hook to attract fish

barb sharp spike

cast use a rod to launch the line, hook and bait into the water

cinch knot knot used for tying the hook onto the line

float small floating object that is attached to the line to catch fish near the surface

fly artificial insect made from feathers, fur or wire used to attract fish

freshwater water that is not salty. Freshwater is found in rivers and lakes.

gill slit on the side of a fish's body that it uses to breathe

landing bringing the fish out of the water

licence permit that allows you to fish in a location

lure artificial small fish made from plastic, wood or metal, used to attract fish

reel device attached to the rod that controls the line

rod long pole that holds the fishing line

sinker weight used to take the hook and bait to the bottom of the water

split shot small weight that can be squeezed onto the line

spool part of the reel that holds the line

tackle all of the equipment used for angling

tackle box box with compartments for storing the hooks, flies, lures, line and other equipment used for angling

FIND OUT MORE

Books

Fishing (Get Outdoors), Nick Ross (Wayland, 2013)

Fishing (Master This), Martin Ford (Wayland, 2013)

Go Fishing and Catch Fish (How To...), Gareth Purnell
(Franklin Watts, 2009)

Sea and Freshwater Fish (Usborne Spotter's Guide),
Alwyne Wheeler (Usborne Publishing, 2010)

Websites

canalrivertrust.org.uk/news-and-views/features/types-of-fish-found-in-canals-and-rivers
Find out all about the fish species that you can catch in rivers
and canals in the United Kingdom.

fishandkids.msc.org/en/play/fishyfactfiles
Visit the Marine Stewardship Council website to learn about
ocean fish and how to save our oceans fron overfishing.

www.liverpoolmuseums.org.uk/kids/games-quizzes/fish-olympics
Play the Fish Olympics game to uncover fascinating fish facts.

INDEX